Feedback or
CRITICISM?

Driving Exceptional Performance
and Creating a Culture of Coaching
by Ben Houghton and Daryll Scott

First published 2009 by Soap Box Books

90 Long Acre, Covent Garden, London WC2E 9RZ

www.soapboxbooks.co.uk

We would like to thank...

Claire Davey, Julie Devonald, Joss Farrow, Caroline Flin, Neil Houghton,
Hiran Ilangantileke, David Mason, Joyce McAree, Kylie Roberts,
Rebecca Stevens, Dominic Scott, Martine Snow, Dominic Ward,
Paula West and Michael Wood.

Daryll would especially like to thank his teachers
Dr. John Grinder and Carmen Bostic St. Clair.
The process techniques that underpin this model are
The Verbal Package and elements of 'The 'n' Step Reframe'
(Whispering in the Wind – Grinder/Bostic 2002).
There are also some techniques that we have borrowed from
'classic code' NLP (Bandler & Grinder) and Ben's input
is strongly influenced by FIRO® Theory.

Contents

Introduction & intention

Dear Reader:

Our intention in writing this book is to provide you with a toolkit of techniques and a couple of simple models for driving improvement in performance through formal and informal conversations.

Like most effective interventions, this came from a need to address some very real and acute challenges. In today's workplace, high performance from individuals and teams has become a necessity for a business to thrive. We (the authors) had a conversation about performance discussions; our perception was that many people were dreading these interactions and getting it very wrong. We then discussed it with some of our clients and they agreed.

We realised, as experienced coaches, that we had a lot of tricks up our sleeve that would be hugely valuable to any line manager, mentor, coach or leader in business, so we created a session about performance discussions. We have been fortunate enough to run the session for hundreds of line managers in several 'blue chip' organisations – providing us with even more experience and really putting our techniques to the test.

This highly effective group-coaching session included plenty of discussion and the examples were demonstrated as discussions. 'Discussion' is a word that we find ourselves using quite frequently and deliberately – we think it's important in the context of this topic. It's impossible to drive or coach a change in performance if you perceive it as a one-way interaction.

You may notice that the content of this book tends to focus mainly on the more challenging conversations and difficult messages. We would like to be clear that the process we will cover is as applicable to a five-minute informal chat as it is to a formal appraisal; and as effective for capitalising on good performance as it is for addressing poor performance. The reason for focusing on the more challenging stuff is that if you can handle these more difficult conversations positively and effectively, you can handle anything.

We are not naive enough to propose a best practice, one-size-fits-all solution to this particular type of communication. We are simply inviting you to challenge your current way of doing things and discover some tips and tricks that can work for you as an individual with your own management style. In our experience, the most effective way of evaluating these ideas is to ask yourself: "What would be the consequences of thinking or behaving in this way?"

Because the underlying content of this book is the fundamental dynamics of human communication, most of the principles and techniques are as applicable to any conversation in business; or outside of it.

Lastly, don't take our word for any of it. The only way to assess this is to do it and evaluate the results you get in practice. There is a bit of behavioural flexibility required on your part – you will need to flex your management style to get really great results. If you do we promise that you will be surprised and delighted.

Enjoy...

Daryll & Ben

The reason

At time of publishing we find ourselves in the grip of a global financial crisis with household names disappearing from the High Street and ubiquitous stories of redundancy. Having effective conversations about performance has never been more crucial to business success, especially when the goalposts are moving.

We work for a broad range of businesses and one thing that is consistent amongst all of them is, whatever they do, they all have a process in place for performance management. They all have documentation to fill in and terminology to describe how they rate people (some use numbers, some use words or descriptions like 'achieve', 'not achieve' or 'exceed'). Some measure just what people achieve and some also measure 'how' people go about it. They all do it in one way or another, once a year, twice a year or more often.

In all contexts we can easily demonstrate whatever the process you have in place for performance management, it's as much about *how* you have a conversation as *what* you cover according to the process. Put it this way, it's not whether or not they are able to follow the process that line managers dread about these discussions...

Sometimes the individual delivering the performance discussion may even use the prescriptive process to 'hide behind'. You can't get into trouble for being professional and sticking to the script, true enough; you also can't have a genuinely empowering conversation with that approach.

A well-managed performance discussion is a rare opportunity to have a conversation that's different to the time-critical, day-to-day communication; a conversation that can be hugely beneficial to both parties. So how do so many people 'mess it up' so spectacularly that it ends up escalated or in some kind of grievance process?

A common dynamic that develops is the individual delivering the feedback paying more attention to doing their bit professionally and selecting their words carefully than how the recipient is reacting and what meaning they are taking from the discussion.

A lack of awareness can lead to people saying things like:

"If they react badly to the conversation, surely that's their problem? It's a 'difficult conversation'. They are a 'difficult person'. Surely I could not be behaving in a way that is contributing to their reaction? I'm just being professional."

We (the authors) earn our living coaching individuals and teams. Our intention in writing this book is to share with you some tips and techniques from our experience as coaches in working with people one-to-one. There are some things that you can pay attention to in how you conduct these conversations that will dramatically change the results you get.

We would venture that the way you deliver feedback influences how people react to it – like it or not. They are influenced by the way you behave, what you say and even what you don't say.

We will go on to share with you some ways of discussing even the most challenging of feedback; on both what people do or don't achieve, and how they behave; which is often perceived as a tougher conversation.

Before we even begin, take a moment to ask yourself: 'What's it all about?' The organisations we work with invest a non-trivial amount of time and money into developing processes that work for their

> **The way you deliver feedback influences how people react to it – like it or not!**

business in a way that is balanced and, hopefully, fair. When it comes to having the performance discussion, time is always allocated to have a private, one-to-one conversation. Think about it; it would be pretty unthinkable to send someone their performance review via email.

(Although, in reality, this sort of thing does happen. We have a few examples of individuals being told all of the good news in their performance discussion and any areas for improvement were mentioned briefly and ambiguously or in some cases not at all. They were then handed a piece of paper to reflect upon later or sent an email after the meeting that contained any negative feedback.)

In most cases that we have experienced, the reluctance to deal with issues in a frank and open way is because the person delivering feedback does not feel equipped to deal with the potential 'fall-out' in the form of emotive and negative reactions on the part of the recipient.

One business we work with experimented with removing the rigid process, only to find that the consequence of this was that people stopped having performance-related discussions altogether. The process was acting as a 'crutch' to equip them for the conversation.

The reluctance to be honest and frank is understandable if you do not have the communication skills to deal with negative reactions effectively. It's also pretty obvious that this approach does no favours for anyone: not the line manager, and certainly not the person being managed.

So what is the real intention of this process? If you were to get the best possible result from a performance discussion, what would that be?

In all of the coaching sessions that we run, participants agree that the overall intention of having these performance-management conversations is to achieve an incremental improvement in the performance of the individual. If this is achieved then the knock-on benefit to the team and organisation at large is obvious.

In formal performance reviews there may be a requirement to agree where someone sits within a rating scale and agree objectives, but this should not detract from the ultimate intention of the process.

Once we agree that constant, incremental improvement is the real intention, we then ask the provocative question; does it always happen in your experience? That question is usually answered with a 'no' or a 'not always'.

We are also working from the assumption that, in order to deliver this incremental improvement in individual performance, a degree of behavioural change is often required. Behavioural change seems to be something that people find difficult to address and extremely difficult to facilitate – mainly because of an unhelpful perception about people and their behaviours – something that we will address later.

In the meantime, let's look at why and how it sometimes goes so wrong.

Have you seen the TV programme *The Apprentice*? If not, the general premise of the show is how a group of young would-be executives compete to become the next business 'apprentice' to a famous entrepreneur. In the UK version the entrepreneur is Sir Alan Sugar.

Sir Alan splits the group into two teams and sets a competitive task. At the end of the task he gathers them around a boardroom table to give them some feedback. What makes it good telly is the drama he is able to create. He provokes what we would call defensive reactions by (as well as the trademark finger pointing) making provocative statements. He tells them things about themselves like "You're not a very good salesman" and "You are not a team player." The thing about us as human beings is, if we are told something about ourselves that we can construe as criticism, our 'primal' urge or 'knee-jerk' response is to defend ourselves against it.

Feedback or Criticism?

In the penultimate show of the last series, one contender was told, "You need to be less defensive." Without a hint of irony!

In our experience as coaches, it is these defensive reactions that get in the way of people taking value from the feedback they are receiving. All the while an individual is defending his/herself against the feedback; how can they be taking anything positive from it? As the line manager, it's the way in which the feedback is delivered that can fuel or diffuse these 'defensive reactions'.

Interestingly; defensive reactions can generate a wide range of negative behaviours – arguing, ranting, blaming, sulking, detaching, withdrawing, paying lip service and agreeing when they don't really, distracting, trivialising with humour or bursting into tears, to name just a few.

The defensive behaviour can also exist pre-emptively on the part of the person delivering it – anticipating a negative response and attempting to avoid it.

Compare the following two ways of beginning a conversation about time-keeping. Imagine how you would be likely to react to these approaches:

A: *We need to have a conversation. You have been late six times this month!*
B: *I would like to have a chat because I'm wondering what's going on with your time-keeping, I don't know if you are aware how many times you have been late this month?*

Option B provides far less opportunity for a defensive knee-jerk reaction because it's more conversational and less accusatory.

If people are defending themselves against the feedback, they cannot be taking any value from it. If they are not backed into a corner, you will learn much more from them.

Earlier in my career I (DS) delivered some performance-related conversations with horrendous consequences. When I look back on them now, they were real 'toe-curlers'. I was labouring under the delusion that there was nothing personal about the information I was delivering, and did not understand that people could take it personally or argue about something that was such a clear 'fact'. Surely my direct, matter-of-fact approach could not be causing problems?

> **If someone is defending his/herself against feedback, how can they be taking any value from it?**

Have you ever been in the situation when the person sitting opposite you (probably with their arms firmly folded) is saying, "No I didn't!" or, "Prove it to me!"? Surely the boot is firmly on the wrong foot here? It's their performance. It's their opportunity to improve. It's their career. It's their loss if they want to waste their time and yours 'arguing the toss' or defending themselves over a given piece of feedback. How much better would it be for both of you if the focus is on how this feedback can be used to facilitate improvement?

The nature of 'feedback'

When you take a moment to think about the purpose of feedback, defending yourself against it is lunacy. Have you ever watched with fascination as a small child learns to walk? They tend to stand, take a couple of steps, wobble, take another step, fall and then repeat the process with slightly improved results each time. Within a week or two they are usually walking. At no point during the learning process do they stop and think, 'I'm obviously not a walker, I'm no good at this, I'll stick to crawling.'

It's obvious that it's unrealistic to expect to get everything 100% right first time. There is a degree of trial and error in any improvement. How many things do you do better now than when you first attempted them? Did you manage to learn to ride a bicycle without a grazed knee?

Yet, we somehow become afraid of the 'error' part – we don't want to get it wrong – we want to be seen to do well – we fear performing in a way that could be perceived as failure.

By 'playing it safe' or going out of our way to 'cover our tracks' and avoid being seen as 'failing' we are making failure inevitable. We are depriving ourselves of the feedback that we need in order to improve. The consequence of being unwilling to err is that you are unlikely to improve.

Think about high-performing sportspeople and ask yourself the question; what is the difference that makes the difference in their performance? It would be unthinkable if, when Rafael Nadal's tennis coach made a suggestion based upon an observation of a particular shot, Rafa reacted defensively and told his coach, "No I didn't; you're wrong, you weren't watching properly."

There are several things that are present in this relationship that may not exist in the business world: The athlete or sportsperson is serious about, and dedicated to, constantly improving their performance, so all feedback is immensely valuable. There is no room for defensiveness because the exceptional performer is already imagining how they will do it differently next time. The positive intention in providing the feedback is overt. It's obvious that the coach is 'on their side' – the coach's entire professional focus is on helping the individual to get what they want.

In the case of most successful sportspeople this attitude towards feedback is not limited to the field of sports – it's a way of being that crosses over into every endeavour. For evidence of this, just watch the sportspeople on reality television shows like *Dancing with the Stars*, *Strictly Come Dancing* or *Dancing on Ice*. They often begin the competition with very poor performance and surprise people by making dramatic improvements and making it to the final stages.

Apart from the disciplined approach of an athlete to the task, what makes the difference is in how open-mindedly the sports people listen to the feedback they are given from the professionals. Meanwhile, the stars of stage and screen seem more likely to let their ego get in the way and get defensive about their performance.

Boris Becker is famously quoted as saying: "Feedback is the breakfast of champions." Thomas Edison famously suggested that, before he finally succeeded in inventing the first light bulb – he had found 99 ways not to invent it.

Failure is an illusion. You are taking a temporary condition or a moment in time and making it permanent. The only way to fail is to stop – to give up. If you do something, get a bad result and never attempt it again, then yes, you have failed. If you do something, get a bad result, learn something from it and have the courage to change something, do it again in a different way and get a different result, then you are improving. You don't know how many attempts it will take you.

Most of us have friends who, when we were teenagers, failed their driving test a number of times, before finally passing. Now that we are in our late 30s, do you think it makes any difference how many attempts it took 20 years ago? Not at all! They're now perfectly competent drivers. Did they fail? No – because they didn't quit.

> **If you defend yourself, it's criticism. If you take it on board and do something, it's feedback**

If you defend yourself against feedback and do nothing about it, it's criticism – if you change something so that you will get a different result next time – it's feedback. This is very simple, or even obvious in principle when you have the perspective of time; when you take a longer term view.

And here's another thing that, in our experience, is completely out of balance: in performance-related discussions, how much time do you spend doing an autopsy of past performance and how much time do you spend focusing on what people will do differently to improve in the future?

If we agree that the overall intention of one of these discussions is this incremental improvement in the performance of an individual, how much of the process is future focused? They may have a clear idea of how they have been performing; do they know what they will do about it tomorrow?

We would suggest that you spend at most half the time agreeing what is relevant from past performance and at least half on discussing future development. At least!

The real question is what can you do about it? How can you get the recipient of feedback to genuinely engage in performance discussions as a personally valuable process without the destructive, defensive dynamic?

During a random conversation a few years ago we discovered that we had both read the Michael Crichton book *Rising Sun* and were equally influenced by one specific line. The character Jack Connor (played by Sean Connery in the film) says, "The Japanese have an expression: Fix the problem; not the blame." We now have our own expression based on the experience we have accrued since: Confront the issue – not the person.

Confront the issue, not the person!

Managing preconceptions

As you have been reading this book there are things that you have been thinking about... Perhaps you have been thinking about performance-related discussions you have had in the past, or a particular conversation you need to have in the future. You may even be reflecting upon your own performance-related discussions and how your line manager delivered them.

Either way, we're pretty sure that you are not thinking about where you went to school, your last visit to the cinema or your first kiss. (Until we mentioned it – it probably just flashed in there for a moment.)

Right now you have gathered up a 'frame of reference'. An unconscious, implicit categorisation of things that are relevant to this topic. You have had many varied experiences in your life to date; as you engage in any activity you gather up all of the experiences and knowledge that are relevant to that context.

Our conscious attention is very clever, but it's not very powerful. Consciously, most of us are only able to handle about seven 'chunks' of information at any one time. Most of the processing of information that enables us to function effectively with the world goes on outside of our conscious awareness.

The most effective way to describe this simply is to use a metaphor: Imagine that you are sitting at an old wooden table in an enormous library with grand pillars and wooden shelves. You can hear the sound of footsteps against the cold, stone floor and the occasional ripple of a turning page through the still air. The library represents all of the information you have access to, you can go and retrieve one of your books at a moment's notice; but you can only have up to seven books on your table at once. Once you go past seven or so, as soon as you need another book, you need to return one of the books from the table to the shelves.

Imagine running into a train station late for a train. You will be aware of the boards displaying the platform numbers, the position of the platforms, the voice over the PA system announcing your departing train; and you will be oblivious to the person selling a newspaper on a stand, and the small child that has just dropped their bag of sweets to your right. They are periphery details that fall outside of your 'frame of reference' for getting on a train in a hurry.

New parents will be aware that something extraordinary happens the day their child is born. It's the same day that someone visits every restaurant, coffee shop, department store and shopping centre where they live and puts up 'baby-changing' signs. Surely they were not there the day before? They certainly hadn't noticed them previously.

Our experience of the world is 'corrupted' by the expectations that fuel our current 'frame of reference' and we respond to the world according to our 'frame of reference' – the books on the library table. In other words, we are oblivious to anything that falls outside of our 'frame of reference' and therefore don't consider it; and we are so sure that our 'frame of reference' is correct that we corrupt what's happening to fit within it.

> **Our experience is corrupted by our expectations**

The now famous psychologist John Bargh experimented on his students to see if he could prime their unconscious minds very specifically to influence their behaviour. He observed students walking down a corridor into his office where he gave them a written test that involved making grammatical four-word sentences out of apparently random lines of words as quickly as possible. The students were not aware that many of the words had been deliberately chosen because they were associated with being old. So they found themselves rearranging words like 'grey', 'old', 'lonely', 'bingo', 'wrinkle', etc. These words were embedded amongst lots of other words and were not necessarily specifically linked to people at all.

Bargh then observed the students walking back down the corridor away from his office. The vast majority of students walked out much more slowly than they had walked in. Their behaviour had been influenced by stereotypical words hidden in a word game.

As Bargh continued to play this game he found that students exposed to words suggesting 'rudeness' behaved more rudely afterwards. Students subtly exposed to word tests such as 'strong', 'firm', 'young', 'quick', 'fast', 'sporty' walked out more quickly back down the corridor.

Merely mentioning a word will shift our unconscious attention and influence our behaviour. The more consequential the conversation, the more dramatic the effect of the specific words used.

Do you remember school report day? If you're anything like us it ceased being a scary prospect as it became more and more predictable. They could have photocopied it every year and simply changed the date. It's interesting that your next teacher would usually read the reports of all the kids in your class to 'prepare' themselves for whom they will be teaching during the coming year. Do you ever wonder what the consequences of those perceptions were?

In 1968, a couple of psychologists, Robert Rosenthal and Lenore Jacobson, set out to investigate the effects of teachers' expectancies on the intelligence test scores of their pupils. The study was designed to measure whether those children for whom the teachers held especially favourable expectations would show greater intellectual growth than the remaining or control-group children.

Managing preconceptions

In this wonderfully playful experiment, teachers were given false information about the learning potential of certain students in a San Francisco elementary school. They were told that some randomly selected students had been tested and found to be on the brink of a period of rapid intellectual growth. The findings of this study created a media sensation at the time and led to several remarkable subsequent studies.

A slightly unhinged chap called Doug Williams, overtly motivated by some kind of guilt to 'blow the whistle' on polygraph testing, conducted an experiment for *60 Minutes* (a documentary made by American broadcasting network CBS). To demonstrate the flawed process of polygraph testing he set up a mock situation in a business setting, the offices of the magazine *Popular Photography* located in New York City. It was beautifully elaborate – they positioned video cameras to spy through holes in the office walls and installed microphones that looked like an overhead sprinkler system. They then picked three polygraph testers at random out of the yellow pages in New York City and hired them to test the employees of the magazine regarding the theft of a camera.

Before we tell you what happened, take a moment to play a quick game with us...

Imagine walking into a meeting that you are dreading; maybe the subject matter is contentious or perhaps it's how you perceive the other person. It could be argumentative, political, false, emotive, trivial, fluffy – whatever you find to be the most difficult dynamic. Now see yourself walking into that room and sitting down. How are you walking? What is your facial expression like? How do you sit in the chair? What does your voice sound like?

Now imagine walking into a meeting that you are looking forward to. Maybe the subject matter is enjoyable, or perhaps you really enjoy

20

working with the other person. Maybe it would be creative, challenging, light-hearted or significant; whatever you find the most positive dynamic. Now see yourself walking into that room and sitting down. How are you walking? What is your facial expression like? How do you sit in the chair? What does your voice sound like?

We wear our expectations on our body language and you can hear it in our tone of voice. It's very obvious and we all pick up on it; unconsciously if not consciously.

It's important to notice that communication is not a process that you can abstain from. If you walk into a room with the intention of communicating nothing, the other people in the room will attribute a

> **Communication is not a process that you can abstain from**

meaning to your not communicating based upon their perception of your behaviour. You are always communicating, like it or not – you cannot *not* communicate.

Back to the polygraph testing... In reality, no camera had been stolen, but all three polygraph testers believed that someone had stolen a camera and expected to identify them. All three of the testers identified an honest, truthful person as a liar and thief, and each one of the testers picked a different innocent victim!

In the case of the Rosenthal/Jacobson study, when evaluated approximately 5, 8 and 20 months later, the randomly selected students (particularly the younger ones) exhibited performance on IQ tests that was higher than the scores of the students of similar ability in the control group. Obviously their scores were way above what would normally have been expected of them.

They concluded that students' intellectual development is largely a response to what teachers expect and how those expectations are communicated. Teacher expectations can increase or decrease intelligence (IQ) test scores. If you are a parent this is scary stuff!

This is referred to as 'The Pygmalion Effect' from the title of the book that originally reported the phenomenon (Pygmalion in the Classroom – Rosenthal & Jacobson, 1968), or 'self-fulfilling prophecy'. The concept is beautifully simple: if we expect that something will happen, we behave (unconsciously) in a manner that will make it happen.

And then, when people respond the way we expected them to we say, "You see! I told you they would be like that!" which reinforces the delusion. If you walk into a room expecting a fight, you could be the one picking a fight although you are likely to be oblivious to this and tend to think the other person is causing the trouble.

Being realistic, we are not suggesting for a moment that if you think everyone is brilliant they will be. However, we would suggest that everyone is capable of incremental improvement and sometimes you can

> **If you have a rigid opinion, don't expect to be surprised!**

achieve dramatic improvement; it's a question of how much time and resource you are prepared to apply.

We are definitely suggesting that if you have a very fixed opinion about an individual (positive or negative) don't expect to be surprised. You will constantly see the evidence to prove yourself right.

Although, just to provoke a bit of thought into this, it could be argued that creating positive expectations that may be a bit optimistic will yield better results than a negative, critical appraisal based upon evidence of past performance – especially as so much of the evidence is subjective anyway. If you want evidence of this, tell half of your team that they have been identified as 'high potential' and watch what happens to their performance with no further effort on your part.

Before we go on to address specific communication skills, there is one element of the communication that makes the biggest difference in terms of attribution of meaning...

Mind your body language

We hope that you are beginning to get an idea of how our expectations and preconceptions affect our behaviour, and how we communicate through our non-verbal behaviour, and that you could be fuelling a negative dynamic when communicating with others without realising that you are doing so.

When we run this as a group coaching session, we provide an experience of how we are unconsciously affected by body language conditions. Participants are often astounded by the dramatic results we are able to provoke, even from a contrived exercise in a training session. It's not something that you can observe or be convinced of from reading a book, so rather than explain it, we will tell a story and suggest some things that you can pay attention to.

A delegate on one of our training courses provided the following story. It took place in the boardroom of a Manhattan bank. Fifty per cent of the attendees were Americans and the other half were from the UK. The person presenting was from the UK and at some point said the words, "We have put together a scheme for this." At that point he noticed a sudden change in the body language of all of the American attendees. Luckily, the presenter was aware enough of what was going on in the room to stop and check what had happened by asking, "Is that not what you were expecting?" After further discussion it transpired that, whilst the word 'scheme' in the UK means a plan, in the US it means something quite sinister and underhanded – scheming!

So our question to you is, what did he notice? What was he aware of that indicated a breakdown in communication?

Here is our invitation to you: if you work in a corporate environment with visible meeting rooms – great! If not, go to an executive lounge, a coffee shop, a bar, anywhere where people become fully engaged in conversation.

Find groups of two or more people that are clearly having an enjoyable conversation. Listen for laughter or slightly more volume of sound, watch for uninhibited, animated gestures, smiles or cooperative concentration. When you are satisfied that the conversation you are observing has a good degree of natural rapport between the participants, observe their overall body position in relation to each other. What do you notice? Are they the same or different?

Then find groups that are clearly having a disagreement or a battle of wills. Listen for abrupt or 'clipped' sentences, watch for inhibited gestures, head shaking and confrontational or disconnected facial expressions. When you are satisfied that the conversation you are observing has no natural rapport between the participants, observe their overall body position in relation to each other. What do you notice? Are they the same or different?

> **Observe people's body language in relation to each other**

When someone is trying to evaluate where a conversation is going, in order to equip his/herself with an effective 'frame of reference', they are reading a lot of meaning into relatively few words. As such, they will become even more sensitive to the non-verbal communication.

If you have not already done so, it would be an extremely worthwhile investment of your time to attend an experiential workshop that will provide you with a direct experience of how to use your non-verbal communication effectively – to manage the meaning that others will put on your behaviour.

For now, we will suggest one guideline for this type of interaction that addresses how you position yourself in relation to the other person.

Typically, in a business meeting with two people, the participants will arrange themselves opposite each other so the dynamic looks something like this (Fig 1):

From the position shown it's very difficult for the recipient to differentiate from the information contained in the feedback and the personal communication or opinion of the line manager. If you deliver information from this 'direct' or 'confrontational' position, you begin to personify the feedback. If the individual has a problem with the feedback, they have a problem with you.

Alternatively, if you position yourself differently you can be 'on their side', both literally and metaphorically (Fig 2):

The difference in dynamic caused by this shift in position is quite extreme. It's much more difficult to 'shoot the messenger'. If the feedback is grizzly, you are not necessarily perceived as grizzly for delivering it. Furthermore, it creates a feeling of working together, rather than the opposing feeling of me versus you.

Play with it and see what happens...

REMEMBER:

- Position yourself alongside rather than directly opposite the other person
- Adopt a similar seating position (eg upright, laid back, leaning to the side)
- Pay attention to any shifts or sudden changes in their body position

Fig 1

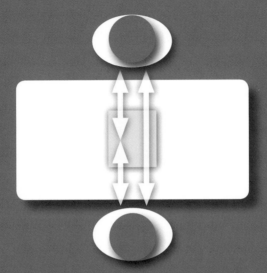

Fig 2

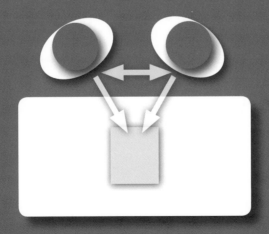

Managing expectation

Hopefully, by now, you have accepted that your perceptions and expectations corrupt what you pay attention to.

Given the importance for the individual involved in this type of discussion it is inevitable that they will be sitting there wondering, "Where's this going to go? What's he/she really thinking? What's coming next? What's he/she hiding?" All of this internal 'chitchat' is an enormous distraction from the conversation you are about to have.

Talking of expectations, this is a quote from an article on performance discussions:

A recent survey commissioned by Investors in People, found that a third of employees think appraisals are a waste of time. The same study found that half the appraised believed their bosses were dishonest during the process, a quarter thought it was a mere box-tick exercise and a fifth thought managers put in no preparation whatsoever before the annual appraisal. (Source: *The Sunday Times* 24 Feb 2007)

We've been working in this area for nearly three years through coaching and consulting and our gut feel is that these stats are inaccurate as they are far too conservative, especially in such turbulent times.

Generally speaking, first and foremost, you are thinking, "What's in it for me?" We're all only human after all. So given that this is what we all think in our performance reviews, why not work with this fact of life and use it to your mutual advantage?

What's in it for me?

If we accept that they are thinking, "How does this effect me?" and you present the information in very professional 'management speak' from the perspective of the business, there is a fundamental missmatch in frames-of-reference; and that's just the start of it.

Imagine going into a performance discussion with someone who has received an unfavourable rating – they may even have received a warning. You are going into the meeting thinking that there is a serious development need and you will need to work on it together; they are thinking, "I'm being managed out of the business."

On that basis, how productive can that conversation ever be? It begs the question: how can you deal with differences in the unsaid stuff?

Here's a provocative question... Why would you acknowledge negative feedback if there is no support to help you address it positively? Surely if you are not feeling supported, or thinking that something positive will come from the process, then your best bet is to argue, be defensive, throw some blame around and get out alive? If something is raised without the offer of support or development opportunity we are back to criticism rather than feedback. By acknowledging negative feedback that is all about the problem, with no attention

> **Why would you accept negative feedback if all it gets you is a smaller bonus?**

to the solution, you have probably gained nothing except reducing your future promotion prospects!

Before we go on to be very explicit about how you can manage expectations in an extremely effective way, we would like to start with a few examples that demonstrate what typically 'gets in the way'.

We were coaching a group of Execs on this topic recently and one of the group said, "It's all very well paying attention to what's in it for them, but sometimes it won't work because of the nature of the problem you need to deal with."

We are always intrigued when someone suggests that one of our approaches would not work so we asked for an example. "Well," she said, "I have a direct report that I have recently inherited; previously she worked with someone else in the organisation. There is something negative in her appraisal that the previous manager neglected to address. I really think she would want to be fully aware of it, and I'm sure I could help her overcome it quite easily, but if I deliver this feedback she will refute it and say 'My last line manager didn't think so' or 'It's never been a problem before'. I'm concerned that she will think I'm too critical and I don't want to get off on the wrong foot with her."

Our response to a context such as this is usually the same provocative question: "What would happen if, before delivering any feedback, you told her exactly what you told us?"

And the penny drops…

Sometimes we can go into one of these discussions with something on our minds about the person or the conversation. Sometimes we might be feeling awkward, nervous or fearful of how someone will react. A way of dealing with this is to be open about how you are feeling before you go on to have the conversation. This has a dramatic impact on the dynamics of the conversation. Like it or not, if you are feeling uncomfortable for some reason, the other person will notice, so you can either pretend and plough on whilst they wonder what you are really thinking and feeling, or you can tell them. This creates more of an open dynamic (being open with them is more likely to make them more open with you) and it removes the opportunity for them to be distracted or distrustful – wondering what's really going on.

Many people in business have a problem with being open. It's another ridiculous, fear-driven behaviour – this

> **This is not a game of poker!**

is not a game of poker! How do you feel about people that you think are withholding information from you? Do you trust them? Do you enjoy interactions that are political, cautious, strategic or false? Are they cooperative, collaborative, creative or productive?

We appreciate that sometimes there is a need to be discreet for legal reasons; aside from that we would urge you to seriously question the need to play your cards close to your chest, and consider the dynamic you are creating when you do so.

Our favourite example to illustrate this is quite an extreme one. Someone in one of our coaching sessions said, "I'm not very good at all this soft stuff. The last two times I sat down for one of these discussions with one of my team it turned into a screaming match. I'm very matter-of-fact in my delivery and some people react badly to that even though I'm just telling them how it is. Most of the time we get on OK and I would really like to have a good conversation with him, but he's just going to think it will be a nightmare again; and I don't blame him for thinking that. I don't know what I can do to improve things and make it valuable for him."

Again, our standard provocative question is effective in this case: "What if you told him exactly what you have just told us?" Frankly, what would be the point of carrying on as if you have not had two screaming matches?

You probably know the expression, "There's an elephant in the room but no-one's talking about it." Well it's the same principle here: all the while you are not saying what you are really thinking, and skirting around the issue, it's glaringly obvious. At the end of the hour you breathe a sigh of relief and tell

There's an elephant in the room

yourself, "I think I got away with it." The thing is, you haven't, since all the time the bloody great elephant was there the other person can see that you are being cautious and holding something back. Consequently, your communication would have been coming across as dishonest or untrustworthy or something along those lines. The other person is likely to be distracted by trying to work out what you are not saying.

The sooner you get it out on the table, the sooner you can begin to deal with it positively. If there is an elephant in the room, introduce it.

It's surprising that people refer to this stuff as 'soft skills'. It would be more accurate to call them 'hard skills'; being 'soft' in delivery creates a collaborative dynamic that allows you to be far more challenging and confrontational of the issues in hand. The intention in being 'soft' is to create the conditions that allow you to be effective.

As a management style, think of it as 'tough love'. By being frank, and at the same time extremely supportive, you can begin to really make a difference. The more supportive you are in orienting an individual with the consequences of their actions, the more irrefutable your positive intention becomes. Be challenging of the issue, and supportive of the person. By the way, if your intention is to point your finger, tell someone off or score points then read no further... This is about what's effective in terms of development and to do so you will need to rise above the temptation to be petty, judgemental or punitive.

Enough of the background stuff, let's be explicit about what we are suggesting and how to do it. As Jed Bartlet (The American President played by Martin Sheen in the TV series *The West Wing*) said in an important briefing, "First let's talk about what we are talking about."

What we are suggesting here is taking the time to have a conversation about the conversation you are going to have. We call this 'pre-framing' because it establishes a shared 'frame of reference' in advance.

> **Pre-framing creates a shared frame of reference**

In doing so we would suggest that you are explicit about your positive intention for the conversation (what's in it for them) and get an agreement upfront to proceed on that basis.

Pre-framing the conversation in terms of what's in it for them at the outset will get them to 'buy into' the conversation. Being explicit about the content upfront will calm the "Where is this going?" internal

> **Pre-framing gets them to buy into the process**

'chitter chatter', and make it difficult for the individual to leap to wrong conclusions.

You are also separating your intent from the content of the conversation. It makes it a lot more difficult for them to 'shoot the messenger'.

> **Pre-framing separates the intent from the content**

If you just jump into delivering the feedback without a pre-frame, it is difficult to separate the feedback from your communication – you personify it, you represent it and if the other person has a problem with the feedback they will probably have a problem with you. To keep a productive and supportive dynamic there is a necessity to be a bit more objective than that.

If you are explicit about your positive intentions for the other person in a way that is frank and genuine, it's difficult for the other person to miss-read your intentions. That way, if the feedback is grizzly, you are not necessarily grizzly for delivering it.

For example, "I need to provide you with some feedback, and before I do, I would like to be clear that my intention in bringing this into your awareness is that I think that you would want to know and I want to make sure that you really understand what it's about. Then we can have a conversation about how I can support you to make any changes."

If I had said this to you, would you want to know what's coming next? As the deliverer of the feedback, who's side do you think I'm on?

In addition, you are 'priming' their attention in terms of what is going to be discussed. Remember the example of people walking at a different speed as a result of the words they have been exposed to.

Anything that you introduce at the beginning of a conversation will prime their experience, so why not prime them with words and descriptions that will encourage a productive dynamic rather than 'management speak' or cautiously selected words that they could easily perceive to be concealing a hidden agenda?

Pre-framing primes their attention

You can save an enormous amount of time and psychological energy if you prime the conversation effectively. If you bought a piece of land to run a car park, it is unlikely that you would open the gates on the first day and tell people to park wherever they like. You would spend time up front drawing out the lines and spaces that will guide them to use the space efficiently.

The most effective way to stop the 'second guessing' and the 'where's this going?' distraction is to prime their attention with something useful.

Lastly, you are creating a frame of relevancy: The conditional agreement of a shared intention for the meeting creates an implicit frame of what is, and therefore what is not, relevant to the discussion. The consequence of this is that it's very easy to challenge anything irrelevant that pops up later if it falls outside of the agreed 'frame'.

> **Pre-framing establishes what's relevant**

If they begin to generate excuses involving other people for example, you can easily remind them that, as you agreed at the outset, it is about their individual performance. If the 'frame' is not made explicit and agreed, good luck challenging whatever comes up later!

One individual in a coaching session found this technique very interesting and was furiously making notes. We asked him for some feedback and he said, "This is great – I now understand why one of my performance discussions went into two days."

The extra time you invest in establishing a shared 'frame' will save you lots of time later and dramatically reduce the chances of costly and time-consuming misunderstandings.

Another manager we met discussed a situation with one of his direct reports explaining that the particular individual was not well thought of by senior executives in their business. He said after six months of working with the person that he had no evidence at all to back up this impression. In fact it was quite the opposite. We asked him what he wanted out of the performance management process for this person. He explained, "Basically, I want other people to see in him what I see in him."

We asked him, "OK, so what's your pre-frame?" to which he replied, "Well I would say to him 'OK; so I want to talk about your performance for the last six months, go through what you think has gone well, agree some development needs and start to talk about where I can help you.'

We said, "Whoa... stop right there! That's an agenda. What happened to the real thing – the bit about wanting others to see in him what you do? How about you start by telling him that?" As often happens, the process had taken over and he had started to outline an agenda rather than his real positive intention for this person.

When you find yourself making a list of things that you want to cover with someone, step back for a moment and ask yourself what your positive intention in covering this with them is? What is it that you want them to take from the discussion that will really help them? Start by telling them that.

If they really don't like the feedback you can even use that to your advantage – they obviously care. Then it's time to say, "If you are annoyed about this, how can we work together to make sure you have significantly better feedback next time?" Alternatively, if you 'flower it up' or 'water down' the feedback and protect people from the consequences of their own actions you are not helping them – quite the opposite, you are depriving them of the opportunity to develop.

When you effectively manage their expectation and you are both 'on the same page'.

And when they genuinely believe your positive intentions for them so that (in the context of this particular activity) you are on their side.

And when they have truly bought into the process and accepted the part they play in their continued, future development...

Then you are ready to begin.

REMEMBER:

- State your positive intention for the meeting (what's the ideal outcome for the recipient of the feedback?)
- Be as honest, frank and open as you can
- Remove the 'where's this going?' distraction by telling them where it's going
- Gain a clear agreement that the intention is shared. (Have they bought in? Do they believe you?)
- Do not, under any circumstances, proceed with the content of the session until the frame of intention is agreed
- Introduce any 'elephants in the room' as soon as possible

The problem with words

Last year we had lunch with Ben's dad, who had recently retired after years as a managing partner of an accountancy practice. He's a soft-faced gentleman with a comfortable air of calm and wisdom. We began to discuss what we were working on, and he listened, nodding slowly as we became more and more animated, explaining how crucial the behavioural aspect of a performance discussion is.

When we finally stopped talking he reflected for a moment and then said, "Yes, I suppose it's that dawning

What you are saying may not be what they are hearing

realisation when you are halfway through a conversation and you become aware that what you are saying is not what the other person is hearing."

We all know how easily misunderstandings happen. For example, if we were to say to you, "We were just being funny," you would probably find it quite easy to attribute a meaning to that sentence. But what did we really mean? Did we mean we were recently being funny; or we were only being funny? Did we mean funny strange; funny ha, ha; or something else?

Here's another example:

Daryll: *Ben, I've got a bit of feedback for you.*
Ben: *OK.*
Daryll: *You need to work on your communication.*
Ben: *OK.*
Daryll: *So you know exactly what I mean by that?*
Ben: *Yes, it's something I'm aware of.*
Daryll: *Great – so we have communicated effectively?*
Ben: *Yes. When we are busy I can take up to 48 hours to reply to an email and I know that people often expect...*

Daryll: *No, no, no. You're not listening. Your communication. How you communicate.*

Ben: *Yes, emails.*

Daryll: *No, team meetings; you need to make your contributions clearer.*

Ben: *Oh?!?!?!*

In the context of performance discussions it is vital to recognise how easy it is to completely misunderstand each other because the words we use are unreliable. The meaning of a word changes with context, or frame of reference.

If someone said, "Your figures are the same as last quarter, which surprised me." Is that good or bad? You have no way of knowing... It could be a nice surprise or a disappointing one. Yet, when we hear an ambiguous sentence like this we rarely clarify it. Instead we apply the meaning that is in line with our expectations.

We often joke that financial statements headed with the words, YOUR BALANCE IS OUTSTANDING, are not meant as a compliment, just as, "That's an outstanding question" does not necessarily mean it's a good one.

As we speak, we have a feeling for what we are attempting to communicate and we choose words without thinking about them consciously. When we do this we're using our personal meanings of the words, which are a result of our experiences (the contexts in which we have heard the words in the past) and our frame of reference for the conversation (what we think we are talking about).

We say these words and they pass through the air and bang on your eardrum (or you read them on this page) and then you do an enormous amount of processing.

Not only are you able to recognise the words as you hear them, you are also able to immediately attribute meaning to those words in real time.

When you attribute meaning to someone's words, you are using your meaning of the word, not theirs. The meaning you have for words are a product of your experiences and your expectations. Other people will have different experiences and expectations, so your meaning could very easily be different to their intended meaning.

We were in a conference room a year ago and there was a sign on the wall that read RULES OF ENGAGEMENT FOR MEETINGS. Surprised to see such an obvious military metaphor, we thought, "What kind of meetings do they have here?"

The third point on the list was ALL PARTICIPANTS MUST DEMONSTRATE INTEGRITY. I'm sure we would all agree that integrity is a great quality to bring to a business interaction. However, if someone were sitting next to you demonstrating integrity, what would they be doing? Can you describe it? What is integrity in terms of behaviour?

The meaning is tacit – you have a feeling for what the word means. We all have a personal meaning for the word integrity, but the explicit meaning is difficult to define. When we attempt to be specific about what integrity is we realise that it's difficult to articulate. You have a good feel for it, but no explicit definition.

Words like integrity and communication are 'nominalisations' – processes (mainly verbs, sometimes adverbs) that we have turned into nouns. Communication is a thing that we do, and there are hundreds of ways of doing it, but we somehow begin to talk about 'THE communication' like THE table or THE chair.

Because a nominalised word can refer to such a wide range of specifics, when we use a nominalised word, misunderstanding is the rule rather than the exception.

What gets us into a pickle is that, when we say these words we DO have a specific meaning, but the word is not specific enough to convey

> **Misunderstanding is the rule rather than the exception**

the exact intended meaning to another person. When one person says 'communication' they know exactly what they mean by that, but when you hear the word 'communication' you use your meaning, based on your expectations, which is likely to be anything from slightly to extremely different to the meaning the other person intends.

As we mentioned before, we are often told that behavioural feedback is the most difficult to deliver. What normally gets in the way of having a productive conversation is how the behaviour is described. It is given a label – arrogant, aggressive, negative, difficult, not a team player. When we use these labels we are sharing

> **Feedback cannot be helpful until they know what they are doing**

perceptions, not facts. You are not talking about what they do; you are talking about your subjective opinion of what they do (which may not be shared by others). This feedback cannot be helpful to the individual until they know what they are doing that is leading to the perception.

Interestingly, factual or numerical feedback may be equally unhelpful. We are addressing the results of someone's actions, rather than what they did that led to the results. The feedback is not helpful until the individual knows what they are doing, so there is a need to qualify the feedback.

Some businesses make sure that they address both WHATs and HOWs - what you are achieving, and how you are achieving it.

However if the what's are simply a statement of results, you are not really addressing what they are doing; you are addressing the results or consequences of what they are doing.

If the how's are delivered at the ambiguous level of perception (for example 'arrogant') you are not talking about how they do things, you are talking about the subjective opinions that are resulting from how they are doing things.

To make the feedback valuable, it needs to be a lot more specific.

We have a friend who was told in a formal performance discussion, "Well we would like to promote you but there's just something about you." Her response was, "OK, in future I'll make sure there's nothing about me."

But a word of caution: when we specify the feedback for the recipient (providing lots of specific evidence) we are falling back into the accusatory dynamic (you may as well wag your finger at the same time). We are proving it to them, rather than helping them come to realise something of value.

If you make a statement about someone's character that they perceive as negative, their knee-jerk reaction will be to defend themselves against it. The more evidence you have and the more accurately you deliver it, the more you are backing them into a corner.

As we mentioned earlier, as soon as someone is gathering evidence or finding argument to defend themselves against a perceived attack, they are taking no value whatsoever from the feedback.

Are you backing them into a corner?

In the next chapter we will cover how to be precise in qualifying feedback, and in the chapter after we will look at the types of language that will manage the dynamic of the conversation, allowing you to be extremely challenging and negate or overcome defensive reactions.

Qualifying the feedback

Here's another interesting and crucial factor that can make a dramatic difference to how effectively feedback is handled. For the most part, feedback is a summary of the results of our actions; "your numbers are 10% down," "you are coming across as aggressive" etc.

Whilst these are the things that warrant our attention, they do not necessarily help us to identify the specific behaviour or action that is leading to that feedback. It's too general or vague to be truly helpful.

Someone's numbers may well be 10% down, but unless they can link that to their performance (what they are doing that is leading to that result), they're powerless to do anything about it.

Someone may well be being perceived as aggressive, but unless they know what specific behaviour it relates to, in what context, how can they possibly know what to change or what to do instead?

If you don't know what the feedback specifically relates to, you have two options: reject the feedback or generalise it out to all of your behaviours in the workplace and spend the next six months being reticent for fear of getting it wrong. Neither option is helpful.

In most cases, line managers are aware that ambiguous feedback is not particularly helpful so they provide 'evidence'. Evidence is an effective tool when it is used to introduce contexts and scenarios for exploration. After all, the intention is for the individual to become more self-aware.

Evidence is destructive when delivered as 'fact' to prove the validity of the feedback and 'pin it on' the recipient.

We're sure you can think of individuals that prefer to give feedback in this way, with

> **It's destructive to treat evidence as 'fact' and 'pin it on them'**

strong evidence to 'prove' that the feedback they are delivering is 'right' – it's obviously not effective. Of course they can present a strong case that backs people into a corner quite effectively. For even greater effect they could shake their head, make tutting noises, waggle their finger and throw in the occasional kick in the shins. Or maybe they could adopt false behaviours, like the falsely compassionate and understanding head tilt and a tight, forced smile as they watch the other person squirm; just an idea.

For feedback to be valuable there is a necessity to get to the bottom of what's really going on and find out what it's really about. This is as true for positive feedback as negative feedback; if your numbers are 10% up – find out what you are doing that has led to an increase in performance. If you are perceived as helpful or effective, what are you doing or how are you behaving that is leading to those results?

Allow us to show you what we mean. In the following scenario we will deliver feedback under two different intentions:

Example one – pin it on them!

Daryll: *I've had some feedback that you can be very aggressive.*

Ben: *Aggressive?*

Daryll: *Yes, it's come from several people in your team.*

Ben: *I'm not aggressive.*

Daryll: *Well, you are. Several people have provided this feedback.*

Ben: *No I'm not. Was it Brian? I bet it was Brian – he doesn't like me.*

Daryll: *It doesn't matter whom the feedback is from.*

Ben: *Yes it does – this is a character assassination, I should be able to defend myself*

Daryll: *You need to pay attention to this feedback.*

Ben: *I don't agree with it.*

Feedback or Criticism?

Daryll: *I have some specific evidence.*

Ben: *Like what?*

Daryll: *Well; there was a meeting at the end of last month that turned into a shouting match.*

Ben: *That wasn't my fault, Dave was deliberately being difficult, and he started it.*

Daryll: *There's also the time when you stormed out of the office.*

Ben: *I didn't storm out – I was getting nowhere with the project and I felt ill so I decided to leave early.*

Etc, etc. etc, Sound familiar?

Example two – lead the horse to water

Daryll: *Hi Ben, how are you?*

Ben: *I'm fine.*

Daryll: *I have some feedback for you and I don't think you are going to like it, but I also think that it will be extremely valuable for you if you choose to work on it with me.*

Ben: *What is it?*

Daryll: *Well before we talk about it, can I just be clear about my intention for this conversation?*

Ben: *Can't you just tell me what it is?*

Daryll: *Yes, and before I do it's important that you are aware of my intention; which is to help you find out what this feedback is really about, so that you really understand it, and support you in any way I can to help you work with it. So on that basis, can we agree to have a frank and honest conversation?*

Ben: *I don't know what it is yet.*

Daryll: *There's no point me delivering this feedback unless you are prepared to work with me on it – do we have an agreement?*

Ben: *OK.*

Daryll: *The feedback is a perception about your behaviour at certain times. The word that has been used is aggressive...*

Ben: *Aggressive?*

Daryll: *Yes, do you have any idea what this relates to?*

Ben: *No. I'm not aggressive.*

Daryll: *OK, but for some reason there is a perception of aggression.*

Ben: *Well ,they are wrong.*

Daryll: *OK, I accept that if you accept that, yet for some reason, this perception exists. So would you like to discover what is happening that is leading people to make the mistake of thinking that you're being aggressive? There's something going wrong with the communication somewhere.*

Ben: *Well, yes, I want to know what it's about because I refuse to accept that I'm aggressive.*

Daryll: *OK; well to help you think of the most relevant situations, it seems to mainly relate to team meetings. When you think of those interactions now, what are you doing that people could perceive as aggressive? How are you behaving in those meetings?*

Ben: *Nothing really, I know they get a bit heated, we are facing some difficult issues and some people are not getting on with it or are making stupid, unhelpful suggestions.*

Daryll: *OK, so when it gets heated, how do you behave?*

Ben: *Well I suppose I have been known to raise my voice a bit, and I do occasionally punch the table, but I'm quite a passionate person. Do people really think it's directed at them?*

Daryll: *It would seem that they do. So now that we know the behaviours* *involved in the dynamic, are you happy to work with me to discover different ways of putting your point across passionately and dealing with unhelpful suggestions in a way that is not perceived as aggressive?*

And so on...

We would hope at this point that you recognised the pre-framing at the beginning of the conversation. In this scenario the recipient of the feedback was particularly resistant, so it took a while for the pre-frame to be established effectively. Notice the refusal to continue with the conversation until there was agreement about the nature of the conversation. If you proceed without an agreed frame – good luck.

Once we have accepted that, for some reason or another, rightly or wrongly, the feedback exists; then we can proceed with finding out what it's really about.

Frankly, it doesn't matter if they accept the label 'aggressive' or not – as long as they accept that there is a perception of aggression and discover what behaviour it relates to.

Notice that the evidence gathered in advance of the meeting is not used to 'prove' that the feedback is correct and back the recipient into a corner. It's used to guide the attention of the recipient to contexts where the poor performance or negative behaviour is happening. Remember the difference between "You have been late six times!" and "Are you aware how many times you have been late?" If you present it as a fact they will defend, if you present it as a question they will become self-aware.

Also notice that the questions are suitably open. There is plenty of latitude for the individual to use their descriptions of their own performance. There is often a tendency to attempt to 'lead the witness' with questioning to ensure that they arrive at the same conclusion that you have decided in advance.

As an example, during a hilarious interview, Caroline Aherne's talk show host character Mrs Merton asked Debbie Magee, "What first attracted you to the multi millionaire Paul Daniels?"

We have heard line managers, HR professionals and even coaches use sentences like, "Don't you think that you are..." or, "Could it be possible that you are..." This is an effective way of softening the blow, but it is still a direct accusation – putting the recipient in the position where they need to accept or reject it. When you impose in this way, you are not facilitating any self-discoveries.

To be effective you need to be much less controlling. As long as they identify and deal with the performance issue, who cares what they call it?

The two questions that we recommend you use to get specific are 'how?' and 'what?' In terms of establishing what feedback is really about, these are the only two questions that you need.

You can also use specific questions to become aware of context like 'where?', 'when?' and 'with whom?' and these can sometimes be effective. However, we would urge you to notice that these questions draw attention outside of the individual's performance – to other people and circumstances. You could be provoking a blame game or introducing factors that they believe to be outside of their control.

To provoke self-awareness of the behaviours or practices that are leading to the feedback, stick to these two questions: what, specifically, are you doing? And, how, specifically, are you doing it?

> **What are you doing specifically? How are you doing it specifically?**

If you are interested in precisely how these questions work, 'What?' challenges the unspecified and ambiguous nouns; and 'How?' challenges the unspecified verbs and nominalisations. In both cases you are moving towards precise and specific understanding.

By the way, have you noticed that we avoid the 'why?' question? People often ask, "Why do you not ask why?" The answer to 'why?' is 'because': reasons, situations and justifications.

> **The answer to a 'why' question is because**

It's really interesting when questioning, people tend to find it really difficult to suppress the urge to ask 'why?'

We're not suggesting that there's anything wrong with asking 'why?' – if you want people to open up and provide their reasoning. However, if your intention is to be precise and elicit more specific information, the question 'why?' is unlikely to be helpful.

When the feedback is qualified, and the individual has become self-aware within the context relating to the feedback, then you are more than halfway there.

There are a few more techniques to share before we leap the final hurdle of provoking real and lasting behavioural change.

REMEMBER:

- Discuss the feedback as the results of their actions and begin to explore further
- Provoke self-awareness by qualifying the feedback – ask them specifically WHAT they are doing and specifically HOW they are doing it?

REMEMBER (continued):

- Use questions like 'when?' and 'who?' with caution – (they take attention away from their individual performance and into circumstances)
- Avoid the question 'why?'

Get out of jail FREE!

We have now reached a point where, in order for you to be able to take this approach, we need to provide you with a few 'martial art' skills to manage the interaction as it develops.

Our experience is that people don't get more involved in these conversations because they do not feel equipped to deal with the 'fall out' of defensive reactions from the recipient. If you just stick to the process and do a professional job it's very difficult to go wrong. It's also very difficult to be effective. Many processes are designed around minimising the risk of bad reactions rather than encouraging good ones.

Our intention is to empower you with a couple of very simple techniques that will maintain a positive, productive and cooperative dynamic at all times. It is the ability to create agreeable dynamics that allows you to be challenging.

We mentioned earlier that these are not simply soft skills – they are hard skills! The soft approach is what allows you to be challenging and confrontational within an agreeable dynamic.

> **These are not soft skills – they are hard skills**

The commonly used approach is what we call 'the s#*t sandwich'. Tell them something nice, then tell them the challenging bit, and then tell them something nice to end on a positive note. There are two consequences to this: they either only hear the negative bit in the middle and the rest was a waste of breath:

You have fitted into the team very well.
There is some feedback from the team that you have terrible body odour.
Everyone likes working with you and you have a great smile.

Get out of jail FREE!

Or they think that things are just fine when you really need them to pay attention to the challenging part of the message:

You have achieved your targets individually and as a team.
There is a bit of a 'clash of personalities' in the team.
I think things are moving forward well and team performance is good.

The body language techniques that we teach and effective pre-framing sets the stage for a productive interaction – with the positive intention established, you should not need to 'flower up' the content.

However, you also need a set of tools to manage the content as you go, to deal with reactions and keep the process on track.

You may be wondering why we put so much emphasis on keeping the interaction agreeable. The following experiment by social scientists Gary Wells and Richard Petty whilst they were at Ohio State University demonstrates why it's an important part of the dynamic if you really want to be effective:

A number of students were asked to help with what they believed to be a market research study for a company that made high-quality headphones. They were asked to evaluate the quality of sound from the headphones whilst they were moving. A third of the students were told to nod their heads vigorously up and down whilst listening, the next third were told to shake their heads from side to side and the final third (the control group) were told to keep their heads still.

They listened to music by Linda Ronstadt and the Eagles, and then heard a radio editorial arguing that tuition at their university should be raised from its present level of $587 to $750.

When they were finished the students were asked all sorts of questions about the quality of the sound and the effect of the movement, and hidden in the questionnaire was the question the experimenters really wanted them to answer: "What do you feel would be an appropriate dollar amount for undergraduate tuition per year?"

The students who kept their heads still were not swayed by the radio editorial; their suggestions for tutorial fees averaged out at $582 year – just $5 away from where it was already. Those who shook their heads from side to side as they listened disagreed strongly with the proposed increase and wanted tuition to fall on average to $467 a year. Those who were told to nod their heads up and down found the editorial very persuasive. They found it acceptable for tuition to rise; on average they suggested $646.

The purpose of the experiment is to explore the effects of nodding or shaking your head. Nodding puts you into a 'yes' mindset and shaking puts you into a 'no' mindset.

What we would urge you to notice here is something even simpler: it is not possible to influence someone when they are thinking 'no', and it's easy to influence someone when they are thinking 'yes'.

To this end, we would like to cover three techniques that can be used to keep a discussion agreeable:

1. Referring back to the agreed pre-frame
If the conversation becomes emotive or strays off-topic and into irrelevant areas, you can reintroduce the agreed frame for the conversation...

"OK, we agreed at the beginning of this conversation that..."

It's never too late to establish a frame, or to refer back to the pre-frame. It's far more effective than a direct challenge to the current content of the conversation.

2. Softening the challenge

Imagine for a moment that it's a Saturday and you need to ask a friend to come round to your house and

> **It's never too late to establish a frame**

move a sofa: you pick up your phone, dial their number and say, "Hello, it's me. Come and move my sofa."

There are a variety of responses this would provoke, not many of which would be positive.

Instead of this direct approach, you are likely to soften it a bit. For example:

"I don't know if you are busy at the moment..."
"I was wondering if you would have time to..."
"Is there any chance that you could..."
"I'll buy you a drink if..."

In our social interactions, we know how to be influential, we know what works, we know how to engage people in our requests. Then we enter the 'process' environment of business and throw away these finely tuned skills that have taken years to learn. With the intention of being expedient, direct, strong, clear and a handful of other misguided ideas, we become un-influential and provoke resistance.

To illustrate the everyday consequence of this, we use a story from Daryll's personal history:

"A few years ago I was working as the MD of a design agency with about 15 staff and, like many small business leaders, I did not have a process of feedback in place for myself. Luckily, most people in the organisation felt quite comfortable telling me what they thought (some with plenty of colourful

language). In this particular case the operations director, a very agreeable chap called Ian, took me to one side and gave me the feedback that my tone was accusatory. I found this really surprising. I was quite an agreeable employer – our staff turnover was almost zero in eight years and I never lost my cool at an employee or penalised them for their actions – I never needed to. I had a coach at the time and we worked on the issue together. After some investigation it turned out to be something quite simple.

"When I asked questions in my everyday urgent fashion, there was no 'framing'. I would appear from my office and say, 'Have you finished that project?' I didn't really mind if they had finished it or not, I just wanted to know either way, but the way I asked the question put them on their back foot. They immediately presumed that I thought they should have finished it, or if they had not finished it there was a problem. I thought I was communicating efficiently and I did not notice their 'rabbit caught in the headlights' expression. This was sorted out very easily with a bit of softening…

"I'm just wondering where you are at with that project so that I can make a decision about…"

"I have no idea where we are at with that project, could you give me an update?"

"If you are thinking, wait a minute – it's they who jumped to a conclusion, they were doing the misunderstanding, they could have easily checked their assumptions. That's true, but I provided the opportunity for them to misunderstand my intention. I could so easily have made my intent or 'tone' clearer."

This approach can be very alien to many business managers and leaders, and they often perceive this as waffle, flowery or just being too nice. If you are thinking this, then we have not done a good enough job of describing the application of the technique.

When you use this pattern you are managing their reactions to your communication – avoiding the negative, knee-jerk reactions that are often provoked by direct and abrupt communication.

This is certainly more effective with some people than others – in some relationships you don't need to soften anything, others you would benefit from softening everything. Also, too much softening can create a 'just get to the point' reaction, and softening something that is quite a soft message is a bit pointless. The purpose of the softening is to allow you to be more challenging.

Again, people often think of these as purely soft skills and in doing so miss the point slightly. Softening actually allows you to get away with being *more* direct, influential and challenging. For example:

*I wonder if it would be OK to ask you to focus on this and **get it done for the end of the day**.*

*I don't know if it would be possible for you to **stop what you are doing** and help me with this.*

Notice from the words in bold – you are telling them what to do very firmly and in no uncertain terms, but they will not feel like they are being ordered about. You are delivering commands under the dynamic of agreement and cooperation.

3. Maintaining Agreement

What if, no matter how well you have set the meeting up, it strays into disagreement? Perhaps, when the content is delivered or the areas for development are introduced they react emotively and begin to disagree? How can you maintain the condition of agreement in the face of disagreement?

This next technique is a martial art. Most martial arts have an ethos of using the energy of your opponent rather than clashing with it.

This may seem a little counter-intuitive, and evaluating this technique from what is written on the page may leave

> **This technique is a martial art**

you less than convinced. We would urge you, as strongly as we can, to do it and notice what happens because it really works and it's a powerful technique.

Here's an example; the person you are coaching says:

"There's absolutely nothing I can do about it!"

At this point you have a choice. You can disagree and they will disagree back. Before you know it, each person will be articulating their point of view in more and more detail or with more and more force and neither person will be listening to the other.

Daryll: *There's absolutely nothing I can do about it!*
Ben: *Well, that's not really true.*
Daryll: *Yes it is; you weren't there when I tried to raise the issue.*
Ben: *No, but there could be another reason for the resistance.*
Daryll: *I know what the problem is – they are being deliberately difficult*

Ben: *They don't think that they are.*
Daryll: *They are.*
Ben: *No, they are not.*
And so on...

After a while one person will 'win', the other will 'lose', or you will agree to disagree. Not an ideal outcome.

Alternatively:
Daryll: *There's absolutely nothing I can do about it!*
Ben: *OK, you're probably right; would it be OK to just check that you have exhausted all options?*
Daryll: *I have, I've tried everything.*
Ben: *OK, I know the feeling. Before we write it off, sometimes two heads are better than one; can we explore some more approaches?*
Daryll: *OK, but I think it's a waste of time.*
Ben: *Maybe – but it's important that we make sure.*
Daryll: *Yes, I suppose so.*
And so on...

This technique works because, by maintaining agreement, you maintain influence and can guide the conversations to counter examples or alternatives.

To disagree breaks the dynamic and at that point you are no longer communicating – neither is listening to the other – they are too busy exploring their own argument, and neither is influenced by the opinion of the other. In many cases, by maintaining the feeling of agreement, you can go on to directly contradict in a way that is very influential.

For example, let's take the challenge, "All business books are a waste of time." There are so many ways to contradict this and maintain influence, please consider the examples below and select the options that you would be most comfortable with:

"All business books are a waste of time."

1. Blending – go with them then turn them
I agree, they are generally awful, and then every now and then you will find one that's brilliant.

2. Go with them and exaggerate
Yes; and all self-development is pointless, I knew everything about business by the time I was 15.

3. Agree then discover a counter-example
That's right. Although, hang on a minute, what about that book by Seth Godin that our whole marketing strategy is based upon?

4. Agree then contradict with a story
Yeah, it's a bit like Religious Education at school; most of it was irrelevant to me, and it was only when I got much older and had friends from different religious backgrounds that it became valuable.

5. Demonstrate agreement with your behaviour then contradict
OK... (nodding and showing that you are taking their comment positively; and then after about five seconds of evaluation)... I disagree.

Notice that in the last example you don't even need to agree. You are simply avoiding the knee-jerk speedy response and communicating to the other person that you are genuinely evaluating what they said before you go on to disagree.

Think of it this way... what would be the point of repeating themselves if they can see that you took a moment to positively evaluate their comment the first time they said it?

This allows you to directly disagree without sparking off an argument. The non-verbal part of this pattern, the pause and the head nodding, are the most important elements to this dynamic.

> **Disagree without sparking off an argument**

If you use one of these patterns with loads of tension in your shoulders, redden in the face and display a tight, false smile, you could get some very unwanted results. You would be better off having a row – at least that's genuine.

To deliver the pattern successfully you are as flexible and agreeable in your behaviour as you are in your language.

As an aside, it would be valuable to illustrate this technique in a couple more scenarios...

This is a great boardroom technique and fantastic for creative and collaborative interactions. If you are chairing a meeting and, as soon as you hear a contribution from someone you say, "No" or, "That's not relevant" – don't expect to hear from them for some time. You have just shot them down and they will not contribute again unless they are compelled to. If you want people to have the courage to express all of their ideas in a creative meeting, validate every contribution. Sometimes the ill-formed or silliest ideas turn out to be the best ones when you work on them, but you need to get them out on the table first!

Have you ever had the experience of someone ranting at you? When this happens, whatever you interject, no matter how helpful, supportive or positively intended, it's like 'throwing another log on the fire'. The next time someone rants at you, let them go... just nod and contribute nothing until they have stopped – they won't go past 60 seconds before becoming very aware that they are ranting.

REMEMBER:

- Soften your questions and instructions (softer and less direct language allows you to be more challenging)
- Acknowledge or agree with their every contribution, especially when you want to contradict (maintaining agreement is more influential)

More handy tips

There is a particular word that will render the agreement far less effective.

"I see your point... BUT"

In conversation, you can hear the 'but' coming. It has an interesting effect on us as a listener. We know that the speaker is emphasising the bit that comes after the 'but' so that's the only bit we listen to. Ever heard yourself saying, "I feel there's a 'but' coming"?

In the case of the example above, use of the 'but' negates the use of the words, "I see your point..." You may as well not bother to say them. To make this clearer, notice how the way that you attribute meaning differs in the following two sentences:

"Your performance overall is good, but there are a couple of specific issues that need addressing."

"There are a couple of specific issues that need addressing, but your performance overall is good."

The bit that comes after the 'but' gets more attention or carries more meaning than that which came before it.

Mind your but

If you want someone to place equal emphasis on both parts of the sentence, you have two options:

1. Substitute 'but' with 'and'
There are a couple of specific issues that need addressing and your performance overall is good.

Or: *Your performance overall is good and there are a couple of specific issues that need addressing.*

Notice that by using 'and' instead of 'but', it no longer matters in which order the two parts of the sentence are presented.

2. Make the statements independently

Your performance overall is good.

There are a couple of specific issues that need addressing.

Whilst we are looking at the consequences of specific words, there are a couple more that would be advantageous to be aware of...

As you read this paragraph, don't think of baked beans. How are you getting on with that? How about not thinking of the 'apple' logo or the sound your computer makes when you turn it on?

When you use a negative, you are introducing the very thing that you are attempting to negate.

What happens when you start a conversation with, "Don't worry..." or "It's nothing to worry about..." The response could be, "I wasn't worried until you said 'don't worry' and now I'm wondering if I should be worried." You are introducing the thought process associated with worry.

Remember from the corridor experiment earlier, how extremely sensitive we are to words. As a listener this sensitivity is heightened because we need to attach an experience to every word in order to put a meaning on what we are hearing. When you use a negative you are identifying what you don't want and then, by saying it, introducing it to the other person's unconscious frame of reference.

Imagine the consequence of starting a conversation with, "It's not a problem..." You have introduced the idea that it could be a problem.

One of our favourite real-life examples of this came from a coaching session – a delegate in one of the groups told us that their boss began a meeting with the words, "I don't want you to think your job is at risk..."

As well as priming people's attention in an unhelpful way, there are some other consequences to using negatives in the context of coaching or performance-related communication.

> **We don't know what we are *not* doing – because we're not doing it**

If our intention is to facilitate a process of self-discovery, we can learn little from what we are *not* doing – because we are not doing it.

Within the frame of a particular context or type of activity, the person being coached can be guided to discover what they are doing or how they are behaving. They cannot become aware of what they are not doing or how they are not behaving.

Let's imagine that the observation is 'not paying enough attention to detail'. It's impossible to become aware of how you do that – because you don't. The most helpful question is, "In this context, when it would seem you are not paying enough attention to detail, what are you doing?" (They could be rushing, distracted, managing time poorly or a hundred other things.)

Some of our clients say things like, "He/she is not exhibiting management behaviours." And when we ask them to be more specific they say, "You know... Management Behaviours... It's a general thing." If you can't specify the feedback it's difficult to drive any real change – it's too vague for the individual to relate to it in a specific way so it's a generalised criticism.

If they are not exhibiting management behaviours, what behaviours are they exhibiting? Start from where they are – not where they are not.

Lastly, setting intentions in the negative is especially unempowering. For example, let's take the common New Year's resolution, "Don't eat chocolate."

All the while the person is repeating these words as a conscious thought process they are making themselves aware of chocolate. (And all the pleasant sensations associated with that word.) They are thinking of chocolate more often than they were when they did eat it!

Some presentation skills training is very prescriptive and draws the attention of the individual to elements of their behaviour that it would be good to stop. They even video you to make sure you have a good visual image of the 'bad' behaviour so you can be very aware of it. This is idiotic. The most effective way to change behaviour is to create experience of what you do want, not draw attention to what you don't.

In the example of 'don't eat chocolate', imagine if the resolution was 'eat more fruit'. You are now thinking of fruit and the pleasant sensations associated with it. You are telling yourself what you do want, so you are a lot more likely to do it – rather than enduring the mental paralysis caused by thinking of what you don't want; fighting against your urges with no idea of what to do instead.

In performance management or coaching, if you alert someone to what not to do you are creating an internal battle and making things more difficult.

Obviously you can use this to your advantage to make positive suggestions and reduce resistance. "I don't want you to think that this can be easy." Or, "I don't want you to spend too much time thinking about the ideal outcome at this stage."

We could ask you to try not to use negative language, but the word 'try' carries with it an expectation of failure...

(Yes we did use a ' but' in the sentence above... we are not suggesting that you banish these words from your vocabulary, simply be aware of the listener's experience when you do use them.)

Consider the difference between the following sentences:

"I will do that for you"

"I will try to do that for you"

Which of the two instils the most confidence? The word 'try' only 'pops up' when the speaker has reservations or is thinking that something may prevent them from succeeding.

Our meanings of words are a result of the contexts in which we experience them... In most cases, when people say they will 'try' they then fail to achieve. As a result, we consciously think that try means attempt, or give it your best shot, but we respond to the word as if it means fail.

When you ask someone to try to do something, you are communicating a negative expectation of their ability to do it – you are encouraging them to fail.

> **"Do or do not; there is no 'try'."**
> *Yoda*

As Yoda says, "Do or do not; there is no try."

Oh, and lastly, by the way... anything that follows 'By the way' is not by the way.

REMEMBER:

- Use positive language (be clear about what *is* happening or what you *do* want)
- Replace 'buts' with 'ands' or 'pauses' and do not settle for 'try'

The problem with behaviour

We have a very consistent track record of provoking positive behavioural change extremely quickly. When we do this, people are amazed and tell us how clever we are. We smile and agree. What we don't tell them is that we are not as clever as they think...

Allow us to tell you a story about a person who worked in a very close team and was deemed by his colleagues to be 'not a team player'. He would keep to his set hours regardless of what was happening in the business, and his co-workers were often required to 'take up more of the slack'. The members of the team were very quick to leap to an explanation of the behaviour – they blamed their colleague's personality, describing him as selfish.

It was some time later when the team discovered he was a full-time carer for a disabled relative – the 'selfish' label disappeared very quickly.

We are very quick to make judgements about the behaviour of others. If we see someone driving at a speed that is reckless we're very quick to call them a name,

> **We are quick to make judgements about behaviour**

and it's often not a very nice name. As I make this negative character or personality judgement, I have no idea what's going on in their world... they could be on their way to a hospital!

It's the result of a kind of something a psychologist would call attributional bias: when we behave a certain way we explain our own behaviours as being a response to circumstances or environment. When we make observations about another person's behaviour we explain it as a result of their personality.

These problematic, personality-based judgements are made tyrannical by the way that many people perceive personality and behaviour – as a permanent condition, as if it's stamped on our DNA.

In practice, changing behaviour can be quite easy. The first step in becoming an agent of change is to cast off the subjective and simplistic evaluations of 'personality'. People are far more complex than these labels suggest, and capable of multiple personalities – one for each of the different areas of their life.

If that seems like a bold statement, evaluate it by applying it to the one person you are aware enough of to make an evaluation – yourself.

Imagine yourself with your boss and pay close attention to your behaviour. Now imagine yourself with a close friend and do the same. Imagine yourself with a family member. Imagine yourself with someone you don't like. Imagine yourself doing your hobby/interest, chilled on holiday or stressed out at your desk or in a meeting.

How many different people are you? And if someone only sees one side of you and makes personality-based judgements on that behaviour alone, how wrong would they be?

People are beautifully complex and they have more behaviours available than the ones they are currently displaying; you just need to know how to find the alternatives.

Another thing that gets in the way of coaching behavioural change is the tendency to think that our ways of addressing issues will be as valuable for other people as they are for us. Dispensing

> **Dispensing advice is unhelpful**

advice, although admirable in intention, is fairly unhelpful in effecting real and empowering change.

When we find ourselves saying, "What you should do is..." or, "If I were you I would..." or something similar, we are telling people what would work for us – and we are probably right. The problem is they are not us. They do not have our skills, experience and understandings. They therefore may not be adequately equipped to follow through on our way of doing things.

More importantly, they may have completely different motivations or intentions.

So the question that we will be addressing in the next chapter is, when we have had a productive and cooperative performance discussion, and we have got to the bottom of what's really going on, how can we effect empowering change with an individual that has a completely different set of skills and motivations to our own?

Coaching behavioural change

Once we have guided someone's awareness towards specifying what it is they do that leads to the feedback existing in the first place, we can then move on to the next stage. How do you coach someone to change their behaviour?

As we said at the very start, incremental improvement in someone's performance requires a shift in behaviour. We now know what the person is doing that is not helping their performance, ie in the example from earlier: raising their voice and punching the table is leading to a perception of being 'aggressive'. The question that needs addressing is; how do you encourage people to discover new behaviours that will work for them in practice, without making prescriptive suggestions? As we said earlier, this is a lot easier than you might think.

It is important to point out that we are working under an assumption here that when considering how they behave at work, nobody gets up in the morning and says to his/herself, "How can I ruin my career today?" (Although a couple of line managers have had to take a leap of faith to believe this about one or two of their direct reports...!)

It would be safe to assume that however someone is behaving, his/her behaviour is driven by a positive intention.

They may be raising their voice and punching the table, but there will be something they are trying to achieve when they are doing so. In other words, there will be a positive intention that is driving their current behaviour, even if the behaviour is ineffective.

Unfortunately, we rarely explore intention in relation to our behaviour.

Let's build on the example from before:

Daryll: *How are you behaving in those meetings?*
Ben: *I know they get a bit heated, we are facing some difficult issues*

*and some people are not getting on with it or are making stupid,
unhelpful suggestions.*

Daryll: *OK, so when it gets heated, how do you behave?*

Ben: *Well, I suppose I have been known to raise my voice a bit, and I do
occasionally punch the table, but I'm quite a passionate person.*

Simply having an awareness of current behaviour is insufficient to
drive change, and making suggestions is unhelpful, so you will need
to provoke a shift in thinking in order to generate positive alternatives.
Whilst someone is paying attention to their behaviour you can ask them
the 'killer question' that will move from introspection to something more
empowering altogether:

Daryll: *So when you are doing those things – raising your voice and
punching the table, what's your intention? What are you trying to achieve?*

Ben: *Well, I just want to get the right decision made so we can move things
forward quickly.*

We have now discovered the real intention that is driving the
current behaviour.

You can notice here that the intention, for them, is positive. The
problem is that the way they are going about satisfying their intention isn't
helping their performance.

This is a pivotal moment in the conversation – when you move the
discussion up to the level of intention, they will become more positive,
animated and resourceful. It is from this point that you can go on to help
the individual explore positive alternatives.

Daryll: *OK, so you say your intention when you are doing that is to get the right decision made so you can get things moving quickly. That's great. Is that what you are getting?*
Ben: *No, not really.*

Note: When people evaluate their intentions against the consequences of their actions, it provides the motivation to change. In some cases their actions will be meeting their intentions, but there will be other unwanted consequences, eg the way they are being perceived.

Also be aware that real intentions are succinct. If the individual begins to explain their intention in detail, it's unlikely to be the intention that's driving their behaviour. For example, if you ask, "When you are behaving that way, what's your intention? What are you trying to achieve?" If the reply is, "I just want to get things done quickly," that sounds like a genuine intention in relation to the behaviour. If the reply is, "To deliver value to customers and stakeholders through reducing cost and... etc," that's nonsense! Our behaviour in the moment is driven by clear, succinct intentions, not mission statements.

Daryll: *OK. So with that intention in mind, how else could you go about things that would better allow you to get what you are after, ie get the right decision made and get things moving and negate this feedback about you being perceived as 'aggressive.'*

At this point, it is worth considering that you are still leading a process of self-discovery rather than telling or imposing suggestions.

Furthermore, have you ever been told how to behave? If you have been on the receiving end of this sort of advice, albeit well intentioned, we would ask two questions: how did it feel and how long did the suggested new behaviour last?

In our experience as coaches, it is far more compelling and effective to work with the individual's intention and ask them to explore alternative ways of satisfying it.

> **Explore alternative ways of satisfying intentions**

It's easy to change behaviour; it's not so easy to change intention. The intention is there, whether you like it or not, and they will find a way of satisfying it. You can work with the intention or against it. If you suggest alternative approaches that do not meet the individual's intentions, they won't last anyway.

Daryll: *OK, so what else can you do that would allow you to get what you want? I agree that getting the right decision made and getting things moving quickly is a worthy intention; how else can you go about it?*

Ben: *Well, I suppose I can begin to:*

• *Keep calmer, count to 10 and put my point across more slowly*

• *Experiment with different ways of explaining myself*

• *Maybe influence the agenda for the meetings*

• *Spend some time with key people in one-to-one sessions prior to the meetings.*

Daryll: *Great, yes I think that will work in meetings. I can give you some help in those situations if you like – maybe give you some immediate feedback?*

Ben: *OK, great.*

It is at this point that you can help them to evaluate what they come up with as alternatives adding in the benefit of your experience.

The individual is far more likely to deliver the new behaviours since they have come up with them, and they will continue to take responsibility for their development.

REMEMBER:
- When you have qualified a specific behaviour, discover the personal intention driving it
- Ask, "When you are doing X, what's your intention? What are you trying to achieve?"
- Once you have established the intention, explore alternative approaches that meet that intention

Here's a graphical representation of the process steps involved in coaching behavioural change (assuming that an effective and agreeable 'frame' has been set for the discussion and the agreement and cooperative dynamic is maintained throughout):

1. PRE-FRAME

Set a frame of positive intention for the conversation and gain agreement. Maintain this agreement throughout the process.

2. FEEDBACK

Explore the feedback as perceptions and results of actions. Discover the relevant contexts.

4. INTENTION

Discover the driving intention: What's important? What are you trying to achieve?

3. BEHAVIOUR

Specify what's really going on: What are you doing? How are you doing it?

5. OPTIONS

Evaluate intention versus consequence and generate alternatives: Is there another way?

Coaching new behaviours

As we said early on, having effective conversations about performance has never been more crucial to business success, especially since the goalposts are moving so frequently.

One of our clients was recently talking about the 'credit crunch' (now there's a nominalisation if I ever heard one!). She was saying that there are plenty of opportunities in the current market – you just have to think and act differently.

Many of today's workforce is younger than 35 and have therefore never encountered a downturn in the economy before (you may be one of them). This is a good example of a situation where, as a business, you probably need to help people develop new attitudes and behaviours to succeed.

We are often asked about how you can make company values and intentions real for people. Companies set out with what they consider to be very important values and intentions, and often struggle to make them a reality for employees in going about their day-to-day roles. So how do they go wrong?

We have already discussed in The Problem with Words section that a value like 'integrity' will mean different things to different people. Different people will have different ways of demonstrating integrity, and very different ideas of what integrity means. Where some companies tend to go wrong is by becoming prescriptive about how employees need to behave to demonstrate a given value.

If we all have different ways of doing integrity then surely the most empowering approach is to allow employees to understand the intention in the value and then 'do' their own version of it?

The alternative is to specify the value in terms of behaviour and tell someone

Find their way of doing it

precisely how to do it. This is highly ineffective since specific behaviours can be delivered in a very unconvincing way if they have not embraced the intention behind it.

If your value or intention is being 'friendly' and this is delivered as a specific instruction like 'smile', imagine how unconvincing this smile could be when it's a forced behaviour.

There is a classic scene in the Steve Martin film, *Planes, Trains and Automobiles* that illustrates this perfectly. Weary after a delayed and overly long flight, and having spent two hours searching parking lots for a non-existent rental car, and then narrowly escaping death when walking back to the terminal across a runway, Steve Martin's character returns to the car rental desk. By this stage it is clear that he is exasperated.

After being made to wait at the front of the line, he is greeted by a lady who takes a look at his angry expression, momentarily frowns with worry and then breaks into the obligatory, false company smile and salutation: "Welcome to Marathon (car rental) how may I help you?" Steve Martin's character responds by verbally 'venting his spleen' in a way that will live on in comedy history for years to come. This loses a little in translation; if you have a minute check out the clip, it's easy to find online.

The point being: imagine Steve Martin's character being met by someone who had been given the intention of being 'welcoming' and was able to do that in their own way, comfortably and genuinely. How could she have greeted him in a more convincing way? Would less prescriptive instructions have allowed her the latitude to recognise and react more effectively to Steve Martin's obvious mood?

By setting a value and then specifying the behaviour associated with it, we are losing the value of the value. The great thing about ambiguous values is that they communicate intention and provide flexibility; there are hundreds of ways to achieve them. As soon as we become prescriptive we are telling people not to think for themselves, stifling any individuality and creativity.

In management, and in coaching, ambiguity is extremely empowering. You may be familiar with the following management story:

A foreman on a building site asks a labourer to "go to the green shed and get a ladder." The labourer goes to the green shed and, upon finding there is no ladder, returns to report back to the foreman.

"OK," says the foreman, "go to the blue shed and get me a ladder." The blue shed also happens to be empty of ladders, so the labourer returns to the foreman once more.

"For heaven's sake!" explodes the foreman, "do I have to do everything myself?"

Imagine if the original instruction was, "Find me a ladder from somewhere, I think that there may be one in the green shed." Upon discovering a lack of ladders in the green shed, the labourer would continue to look elsewhere.

If the people you are managing have no idea of your intention they are unable to do anything but respond to your specific instruction; if they cannot complete the instruction exactly as asked, they become stuck. You have communicated what to do but not how to think.

> **Ambiguity can be extremely empowering**

If people understand your intention and cannot fulfil your instruction, they can think for themselves.

However, this ambiguity needs managing – otherwise individuals will have no idea what's expected of them and the values may seem like nonsense.

Sometimes company values are coined in the boardroom and are very relevant there, but they are less accessible, or less realistic, on the front line.

We heard a story a couple of years ago about a lady who carries out mystery shopping for a chain of fast-food restaurants. Our mystery shopper had a list of the usual specific observations to make: was the counter clean? How long did it take to get served? Did they get the order correct?

Somewhere in the list was the question, "Was the person who served you passionate?" I wonder how they could be passionate about fast food? You would probably be a bit unnerved if they were.

I'm sure it was a good idea in the boardroom. The intention of wanting people to be passionate is certainly positive for the individuals who work within the business, and passionate employees are likely to improve the performance of the business at large. The question is: how can you ensure that this translates to the front line in a way that is accessible, genuine and convincing?

We demonstrated earlier that a word like 'integrity' has no explicit meaning. This lack of clarity can be confusing. On the other hand it can be extremely empowering as it provides the latitude for an individual to employ their natural and individual behaviours to meet that intention or value.

Our intention is to show you a compelling process to coach someone to discover his/her own behaviours that support a company value or high-level intention.

If you are using values to coach performance, there is a necessity for the individual to discover their own meaning of the value and a way of doing it that works. We have used the following process for individual coaching and in workshops to great effect. We find there are several stages that we list below in turn.

What's the context?
In exploring behavioural change under broad, nominalised words it's important to have a frame of reference so that you can be specific and evaluate changes. In this process, the 'frame' is provided by the context, so we work with one at a time.

For example you may explore a value in the context of presentations, then in meetings, then in networking scenarios. It is necessary to do this one context at a time. To attempt to evaluate your behaviour in all contexts simultaneously is overwhelming and it's almost impossible to be precise.

Let's use a couple of examples:

Example 1: Let's imagine that a hospitality company has realised one of the things that will enhance their customer's experience is how warmly they are welcomed, so the value or intention is being welcoming. The context could be when the customer first arrives at the venue.
Example 2: Imagine a B2B environment where the high-level intention is being responsive. The context is identified; let's say responding to calls from clients.

What do they do currently?
Using the techniques that we demonstrated earlier, qualify the individual's current behaviour: what are they doing? How are they behaving?

The intention is for the individual to have a very specific awareness of their behaviour within the context that you are working.

What does this value mean to you?

Values are by their very nature ambiguous and before we can begin to use them to drive behavioural change, we must first explore the meaning that the person is putting on the value to check it is generally in line with the intention of the organisation.

Simply ask them what they think it means. Using the example of 'welcoming', notice that for some mild mannered individuals their version of being welcoming does not necessarily involve a big cheesy smile.

For some people, 'responsive' is about speed, for others it's about listening to the client and getting back to them with the right thing.

Some people will misunderstand the value completely. An effective way of providing a resourceful perspective is to ask, "What do you think the intention of the value is?"

Find their way of doing it

The next part of this process takes advantage of the fact that people already have far more behaviours at their disposal than those they demonstrate just at work.

Take being welcoming for example; ask them to think of any context in their life where they are really welcoming. Encourage them to imagine themselves in any context where they are – it might be greeting friends when they come round to their house, when they meet them for a coffee, or at the beginning of a night out.

As they imagine themselves in that context, ask the person to notice what they do when they are being extremely welcoming. They are now imagining another set of behaviours that are different to the ones that they observed at the first stage of this process (the existing behaviour in the work context).

They might observe themselves making eye contact, having much more open body language, feeling more energetic, being a bit more attentive and so on. We now have some real behaviours that we know are available to that person, albeit in another context.

For 'responsive' the other context could be playing sport, driving a vehicle, hosting the pub quiz, playing a challenging video game, and arranging a night out with friends, and you can then specify the behaviour in any of those contexts quite easily.

Compare and contrast

We now ask the person to compare and contrast the behaviours they know they demonstrate in the other context with those in the work context. You can then encourage them to imagine the behaviours from the new context (eg arranging a night out) in the original context (eg handling a customer call).

An example question that will work very nicely is: "When you think of those behaviours that you do so well in other areas of your life, what would it be like if you were to behave more like that in this particular work context?"

By the way, there is a little bit of mind-trickery going on here as well. By visualising the more resourceful behaviours at work they are teaching themselves unconsciously how to do it.

Evaluate the additional behaviours

You can encourage them to give examples of what they would do differently and how they would behave if they map these additional behaviours into the work context. From the welcoming example we may end up with something like:

'I will make more eye contact.'
'I will be more open in my body language.'
'I think I will be patient and take more time to focus on each customer as an individual.'

These discoveries can provide a very powerful tool for future performance discussions. You will be coaching on behaviours that you know they can do and because they have suggested them, they will own the process.

Obviously some behaviour that we exhibit in our social life may be a little inappropriate or may not work for us in a commercial context. This provides you with an opportunity as the coach to help them evaluate their additional behaviours from the criterion of whether they are likely to be effective.

Realising the difference in your body language when you are more engaged at work can be a revelation; pinching people on the bottom may get you some unwanted results!

This process is compelling since it is using behaviours that the person already has an effective way of doing (a strategy). We are simply using a process to map the strategy from one part of their experience to another. They are far more likely to be able to do these behaviours since they are already their own. We have created an experience that allows them the flexibility to be themselves, deliver against intentions and/or reflect company values in how they behave.

1. PRE-FRAME

Set a frame of positive intention for the conversation and gain agreement. Maintain this agreement throughout the process.

2. FEEDBACK

Identify the area of activity that this process is being applied to.

4. 2ND CONTEXT

Identify when the individual does the value or intention naturally.

3. BEHAVIOUR

Specify what's really happening:
What are you doing?
How are you doing it?

5. 2ND BEHAVIOUR

Specify the new behaviour:
What are you doing?
How are you doing it?

6. NEW BEHAVIOURS

Compare behaviours (3) and (5).
Evaluate 2nd behaviours (5) in original context (1).
What would be different?

REMEMBER:

- Identify the area of activity you are addressing and the positive intention for that activity
- Find examples where the individual does meet that intention in any activity (hobbies/interests/social life)
- Find out how they behave in those example scenarios (be very specific)
- Evaluate those specific behaviours in the original area of activity that you are working on

The End

That brings us to the end of our little journey into developing a 'coaching mentality' towards performance. We hope that you enjoyed this book and that it will encourage you to use these techniques; you will find that they can be dramatically effective.

We welcome your questions and invite your feedback. You can contact us directly via our personal email addresses:

- Ben@mynoggin.co.uk
- Daryll@mynoggin.co.uk

For more information about this and other activities, please visit:

www.mynoggin.co.uk